Copyright © 2024-2025 by Pippa Bird

All rights reserved. No part of this book may be reproduced or transmitted in any form or by any means, electronic or mechanical, including photocopying, recording, or by any information storage and retrieval system, without permission in writing from the publisher.

ISBN: 9781763833876

First Edition

Pippa Bird
Kind Kookaburra

In the heart of the Australian bush, there lived a kookaburra named Cookie. He was part of a large family. And while they all looked and sounded very similar, Cookie couldn't help but feel different.

One morning, Cookie's family was laughing loudly at a joke. He tried to join in, but he just didn't find it funny.

Cookie had a more gentle and thoughtful nature.

One of Cookie's family members turned to him and said, 'Why aren't you laughing? It's funny. You *should* be laughing like the rest of us.'

'I didn't find it funny!' exclaimed Cookie.

The rest of Cookie's family started laughing louder.

Feeling out of place and a little sad, he flew to his favourite quiet spot by the river.

Cookie sighed, 'I feel different from my family. They laugh at things that I don't find funny. I feel like I don't belong.'

'It's okay to be different, Cookie. Your kindness and calm nature are what make you special. You don't have to be like everyone else to be lovable. You are lovable just as you are,' said Kirri, softly.

Later that morning, Penelope Platypus swam upstream.
'Oh my dear friend, Cookie, what is the matter?'

Cookie explained his feelings, and Penelope nodded. 'Being different is what makes the world interesting. Imagine if everyone was the same. Your family loves you for who you are, even if you don't laugh at the same things.'

Cookie sat in his favourite place, thinking about what his friends had told him.

'Why do you look so thoughtful, Cookie?' asked Esmeralda, as she strolled by.

Cookie shared his feelings, and Esmeralda smiled. 'I understand how you feel. I sometimes feel different too. But I've learned that being different is okay. It makes us unique and special.'

'But some of the things my family laugh about are mean. I don't know how to feel about it,' whimpered Cookie. 'It's confusing.'

Cookie flew from the tree. He found his emotions too overwhelming to sit still. He didn't know how to feel. He didn't know what to think.

As the kookaburra landed in another tree, a friendly old tortoise strolled over.

'Oh Cookie, my dear, why do you look so sad?' asked Tallulah.

Cookie sighed and began telling her his story.

The other bush friends gathered to support Cookie again. They came to listen and share their empathy.

'Remember what we told you, Cookie,' said Kirri. 'You don't have to be like everyone else to be lovable. You are lovable just as you are.'

'Your family loves you for who you are, even if you don't laugh at the same things,' said Penelope.

'And being different is okay. It makes us unique and special,' said Esmeralda.

With his bush friend's support, Cookie began to see his differences in a new light. He realised that his kindness was his strength, and he didn't need to be the same as his family to feel like he belonged.

'Perhaps you could talk to your family about how you're feeling. It may help them to understand your perspective.'

Cookie nodded softly.

A little afraid, but more determined, Cookie flew back to his family.

Cookie expressed his emotions to his family, explaining how some things made him feel uneasy, sad or confused. And that he felt as though he didn't belong.

'No more mean jokes that aren't funny,' followed his brother.

Cookie's sister spoke up. 'We understand, Cookie. And we never intended for you to feel this way. We are sorry. We love you and only wish for you to be happy.'

As the sun began to retire and stars sprinkled the sky, Cookie and his family took flight.
Kindness had become their compass, and together they embraced their new bond.

Introducing Calm Kangaroo's Mindfulness & Wellbeing Journal: 10 Week Program

Research highlights that mindfulness journaling can significantly improve emotional regulation in primary-school aged children, resulting in better mood stability, reduced anxiety, and stronger self-awareness. This journal is designed to support the same benefits, giving young minds the space to reflect, reset, and grow - one mindful moment at a time.

Baourda, V. C., Brouzos, A., & Vassilopoulos, S. P. (2024). "Feel Good-Think Positive": A Positive Psychology Intervention for Enhancing Optimism and Hope in Elementary School Students. A Pilot Study. International Journal of Applied Positive Psychology, 9(2), 1105-1125.

Devcich, D. A., Rix, G., Bernay, R., & Graham, E. (2017). Effectiveness of a mindfulness-based program on school children's self-reported wellbeing: A pilot study comparing effects with an emotional literacy program. Journal of Applied School Psychology, 33(4), 309-330.

This delightful adventure invites children to explore mindfulness and self-care with weekly wellbeing check-ins and self-reflections, mindfulness colouring and expressive art activities

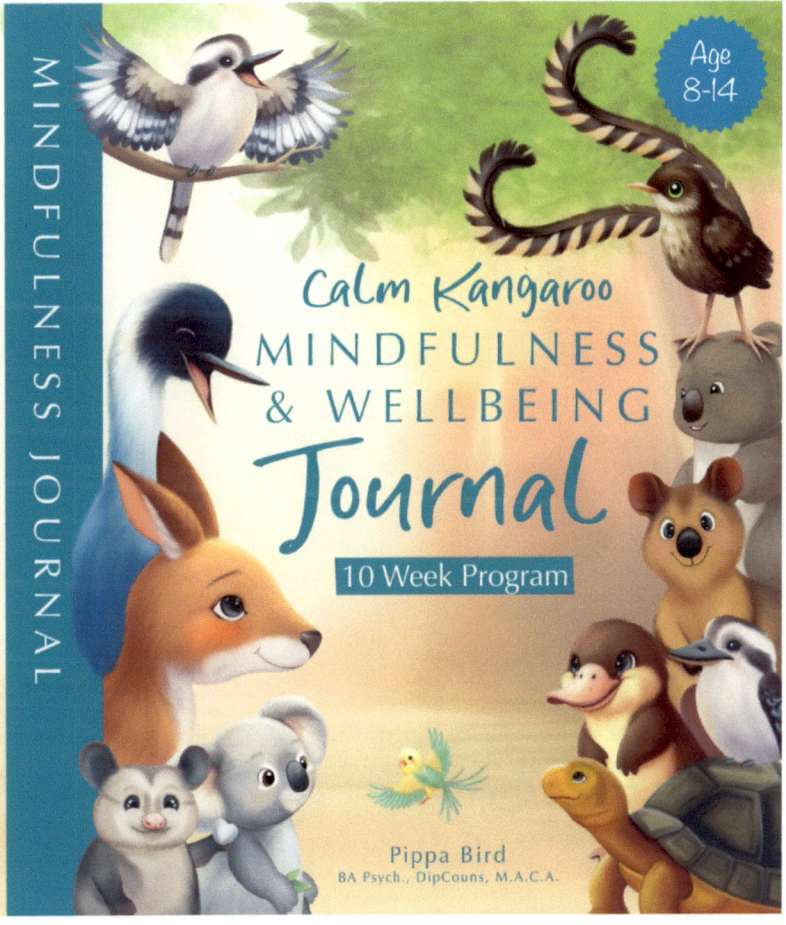

Available on Amazon

www.ingramcontent.com/pod-product-compliance
Lightning Source LLC
LaVergne TN
LVHW072118070426
835510LV00003B/119